Contents

Introduction to the pack

Welcome to the organisational skills pack for schools. Gaining good organisational and time management skills are essential for all children and adults in order for them to plan, complete and finish tasks in home, school and eventually the workplace.

This pack contains a range of practical strategies to start off this process.

Different students may require different approaches; there will not be one technique that suits all students. For example using visual timetables may help some students who have a good visual memory. Using audio tapes to hear work may help other students with good listening skills.

Adequate practice is required when trying any new technique. Some students may not be developmentally ready to try some approaches, so try again after a period of time.

Visual Timetables

Visual timetables allow the student to see, with pictures/words, how to organise themselves and their day. These pictures/words can be further broken down into individual lesson plans or used for a daily or weekly timetable.

Ideas to help:

- Ask the students to find or draw pictures for each of their subject areas. There are also pictures of these included in the pack.
- Pictures could be taken using a digital camera or could be drawn on the computer, found on the internet or drawn by hand.
- These could then be laminated or covered in "Contact" (plastic covering). Attach Velcro to the back of the cards. These can then be attached to a board or firm card with the other side of the Velcro strip. As each subject or task is completed, the student can remove the picture and place it in a 'done' folder or an envelope.
- Alternatively a strip of card can be used and placed on the desk in front of the student.

- analogue or digital clock pictures with different times showing can also be made and placed alongside each task to allow the student to see how long the task should take and when to move on to the next task.

An example of a visual timetable

Calendar

A calendar can be useful for letting the students know what is planned during the week/month allowing them to prepare. It can help to remind the students of important events (tests, outings).

This can potentially reduce anxiety levels for the student. It can also be useful for reinforcing time and date concepts. It provides opportunities for teaching specific time-related terminology (e.g. before, after, fortnight, next, yesterday).

Ideas to help:

Pictures rather than words may need to be used with younger children (see back of this pack for templates). Using pictures alongside words may help to reinforce reading and spelling skills, as well as improving organisational skills.

- A calendar with enough space to write events for each day should be placed in a prominent position in the classroom.
- Individuals could make their own calendar on the computer or by hand and write in their activities such as sports matches, homework.

- Remind the student to update their calendar once a week on a regular day.
- Students should be reminded daily to look at their calendar for any events happening that day, or events further on in the week that they may need to prepare for. This makes it into a routine task.

For example:

MONDAY	TUESDAY	WEDNESDAY	THURSDAY	FRIDAY
1	2	3	4	5 Assembly
6 Trip money due	7	8	9 Non uniform day	10 Assembly
11	12	13	14	15 Assembly
16	17	18	19	20 Assembly
21	22 SCHOOL BUS School Bus	23	24	25 Assembly

Homework Planning

Getting homework down at the end of the lesson may be more challenging for students who have difficulty with their handwriting. Students may be slower recording their work or their handwriting may become illegible when writing at speed. If the homework is inaccurately recorded or illegible the student may not complete the correct piece of work or just not do any of the homework, potentially getting into trouble.

Ideas to help:

- Homework could be printed on to sticky labels so that the student can just "peel" them off the sheet and place them in their homework diary. Alternatively you could use sheets of paper that the student can place in a homework book.
- Allocate a young person to record homework for a buddy who is having difficulties. Carbon paper could be used to make double copies.
- Write homework on the whiteboard at the start of the lesson so that the student has more time to copy it down.
- Allow specific allocated time at the end of a lesson to write homework down (not when the student is packing up and is distracted).

- Consider setting up a school intranet homework site so that students and parents can access the information at the end of the day.

- Allocate a buddy who can send the homework via e-mail or by using MSN® Messenger or an equivalent service provider. Young people with specific learning difficulties in particular may not have the same network of friends and as a result do not have the ability to "just make a call" or go on MSN® for a chat. This may need to be more formally set up between home and school.

- A Dictaphone or small pocket recording device could be used for recording homework. Key-ring voice recorders are often available from Boots® or NEXT® for example.

- If the student uses a computer or Pocket PC this could record the timetable and the homework so it remains "filed" all in one place.

- In schools where mobile phones are allowed, many have the ability to write down to-do lists. Students can often be quick at texting and so may be able to do this faster than writing by hand.

To-do Lists

To-do lists can help the student to think in a step-by-step way and improve analytical skill and keep track of tasks. They make it easier to prioritise tasks and motivate them to see what they have completed.

Ideas to help:

- The student could use a small pad of paper to make the to-do lists or use a shop bought version.
- First talk to the student about a task or tasks that need to be completed. Break the task into smaller steps.
- Encourage the student to then write the steps down.
- Each task should be ticked on completion.
- Encourage students to be realistic when setting tasks on their to-do list.
- Try to show the student how to be specific in the tasks they are setting. This gives the student a clear idea of what needs to be achieved.
- Add an additional column if necessary with an approximate time allocation.

- Review with the student to see if tasks were completed and how they may need to make adjustments in the future.
- Talk with the student about how long a task is likely to take and consider whether this is an accurate assessment.

For example:

Things to do (Maths)	Done
Get out textbook, exercise book, pens and ruler	✓
Do questions 1-5 on page 7	✓
Hand work in to the teacher	✓

Time Concepts

Some students may have poor concepts of time. This is sometimes called "time blindness". For example this may be seen when a student is told that they have 5 minutes to complete a task and then continues to work, unaware of the need to finish. Alternatively some students ask the teacher again and again when the time will be up.

The student needs to learn time management skills because they are essential in all aspects of life. If this is not achieved it will have an ongoing impact for the student in their day-to-day life.

Ideas to help:

Students will need different approaches to learning time concepts.

Some students need to see time passing, others like to hear an alarm or bell. Just wearing a watch may not be enough for the student as he or she has to remember to look at it!

- Use a visual timer such as an egg timer or a timer with an alarm. Find out from the student whether they are better with an analogue clock (seeing time passing by) or a digital clock.

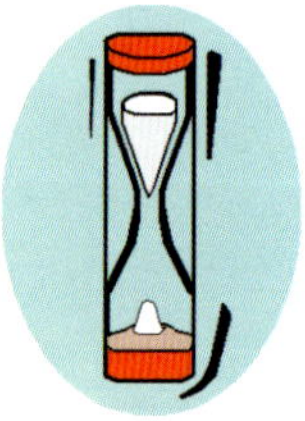

- Encourage the student to use the timer when needing to work to a time limit e.g. 15 minutes. Consider auditory timers that buzz when the time is up.
- With older students, consider using their mobile phones as an alarm/reminder.
- Work with the student to gain concepts of time based on familiar experiences (e.g. give examples such as walking to school takes 10 minutes, assembly always lasts for 30 minutes) i.e. where a time is familiar and can be recalled by the student. Relate a new task to a familiar time frame so they can match the "feeling" until it is automated, such as "You need to complete this task in 20 minutes, that's the same length of time as break time".
- Encourage the child to guess how long a task will take and then build in extra "buffer" time to reduce unnecessary anxiety.

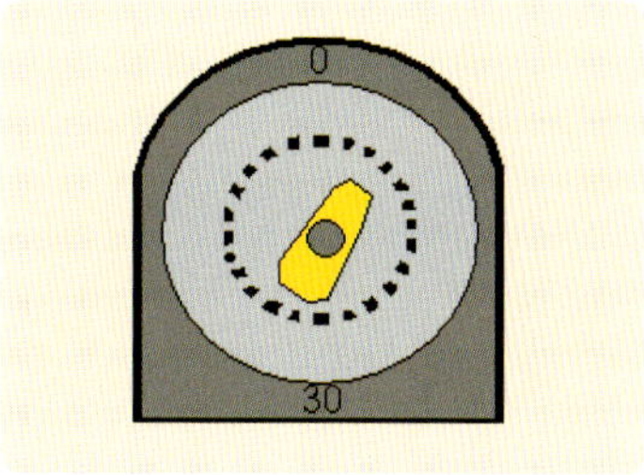

Organising Work – Concept Maps

These provide a visual format for note taking rather than a linear one. Some students may find this strategy really helpful. However this approach may not suit all students.

Concept mapping can be useful for revision (summarising information), note taking (minimising writing), planning stories and assignments.

Ideas to help

- Reinforce the different components when constructing an essay.
- Brainstorming – try using Post-It® notes for the student to record their ideas.
- Organising - arrange the Post-It® notes into groups.
- Layout - arrange the groups into a logical sequence.
- Using different colours to highlight the groups may help the student to arrange these ideas and then create sentences and paragraphs.

Concept maps on paper

- Begin at the centre of the paper or from the top down. Students will learn their own style.
- Highlight the main topic by writing it in bold.
- Draw branches coming from the main topic.
- Then write sub-topics at the end of these. Other branches can then come off these if necessary.
- Use as much colour and as many symbols and pictures as the student likes. It is sometimes easier to start either with words or symbols to get the technique and then add in a second layer of information.
- Don't crowd the page – leave lots of white space.
- Most importantly, only use the key words that are needed to be remembered.

For example:

A simple concept map

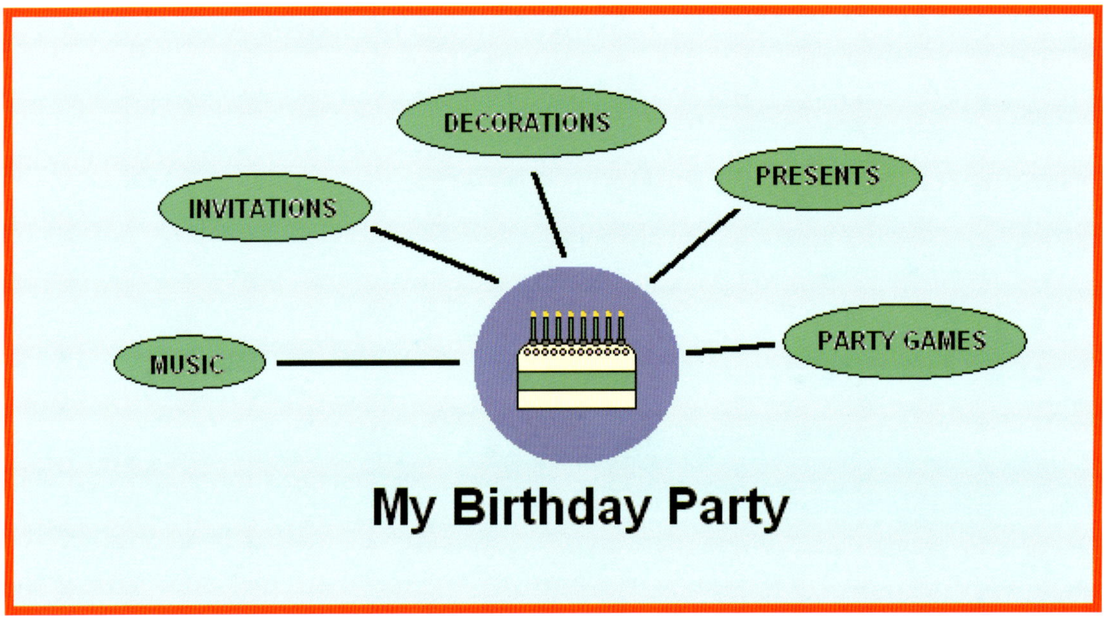

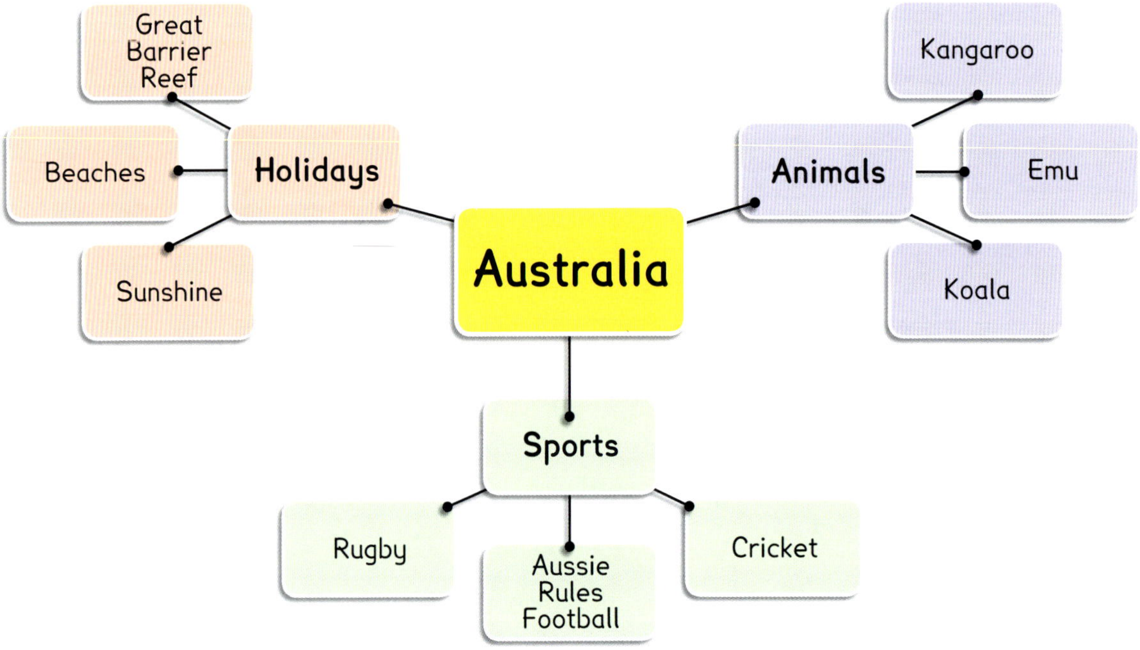

Computer based concept maps – You can use computer concept mapping programmes such as 'MindFull®', 'Kidspiration®' or 'Inspiration®'. These programmes can be purchased from www.dyslexic.com or www.clarosoftware.com.

Question Grids

If writing and drawing are difficult, an alternative approach is to make a grid to put down ideas, for example the following:

Question	Kangaroo	Sheep	Crocodile	Koala	Black Widow Spider
What do they eat?					
Where do they live?					
Fur or feathers?					
Mammal, reptile, insect or fish?					
What do you like about the animal?					

Frameworks For Essays

Creating a template for an essay is helpful especially when consistent information and a style has been established. For example, if the student has to write their name at the top of every essay, number each page and put references in a certain style, all of these could be pre-formatted on a computer and kept as a template for the student to start with. This saves time and ensures a consistent approach.

A useful website with freely downloadable examples of writing frames can be found at:

http://www.warwick.ac.uk/staff/D.J.Wray/Ideas/frames.html

Another site which gives specific and detailed instructions on creating writing frames in Microsoft Word for students can be found at:

http://www.kented.org.uk/ngfl/subjects/literacy/Writing-frames/frames2.html

An example of a computer essay planner is a computer programme called "Stick-IT®" (available from www.dyslexic.com or The Dyscovery Centre, www.dyscovery.co.uk).

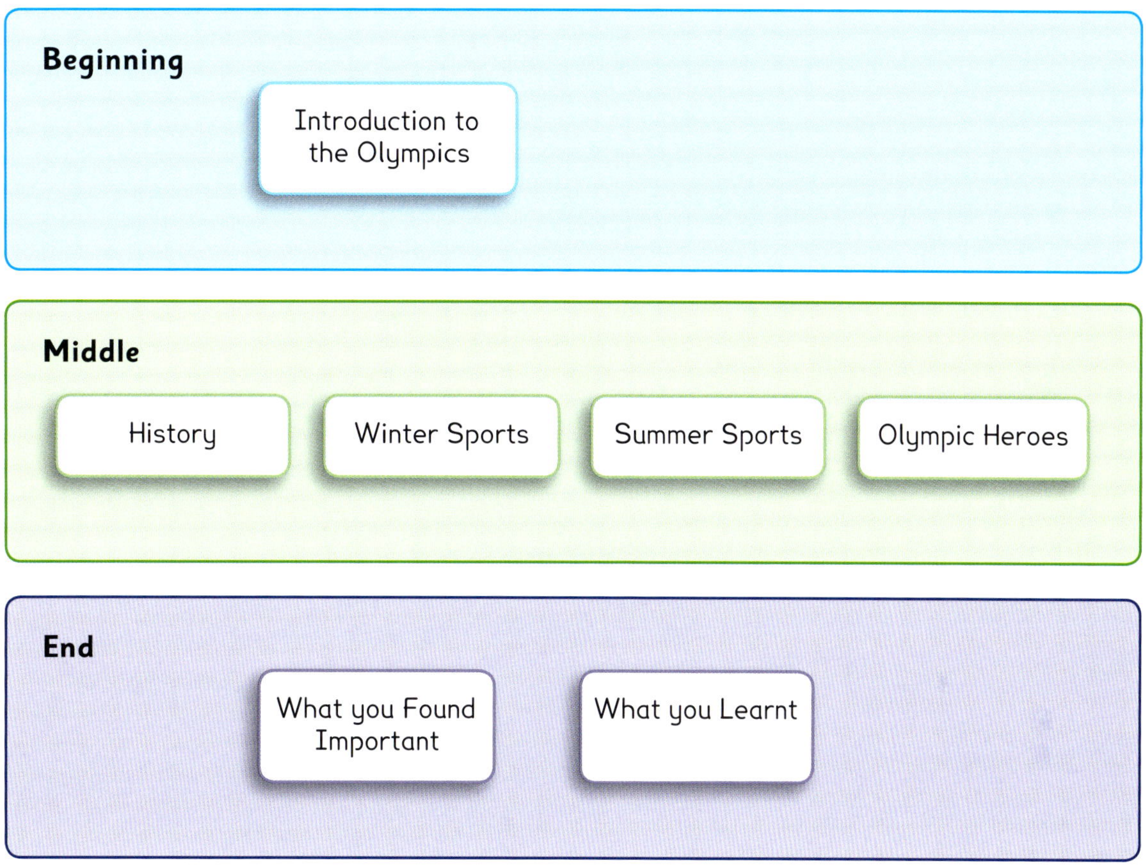

Organising Self and Possessions

It can be both stressful and costly for students to regularly lose their possessions. They can also waste lots of time looking for items. Carrying out regular routines for storing items can save time and effort e.g. always putting pencils and pens in one drawer after using them. If this is done often enough it will become automatic so the student doesn't have to think about it.

Ideas to help:

- First talk with the student to identify what he or she needs to organise, such as stationery items, books or folders, sports clothing.
- Use clear plastic boxes, Tupperware® containers or clear pencil cases for small items so they can be easily seen and checked. Keep a list of the items inside the pencil case so the student can check items back into the case at the end of every lesson.

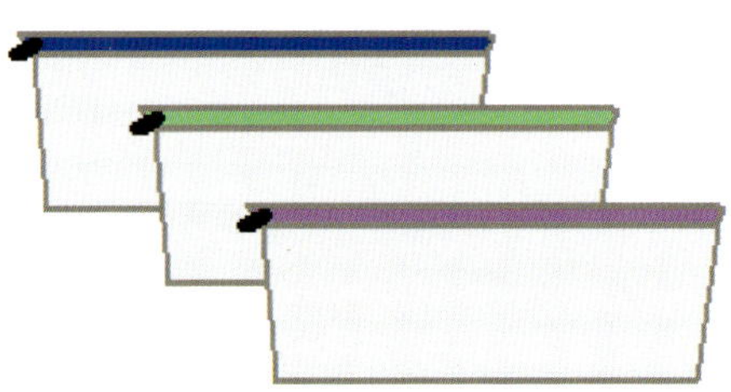

- When labelling each container try using pictures, photos or words of the items being stored. Different coloured containers offer an additional aid to remembering where specific items are kept e.g. blue for pens and green for rulers and rubbers.

- Always place items back in the same place for consistency.
- Encourage students to have a spare pencil case at home so the school one stays in their school bag. This reduces the risk of losing items or leaving them behind.
- Separate notes into files or in folders using coloured tabs such as those made by Post-it®. These can be stuck on and removed but make it easier for the student to find relevant pages they are working on.
- Supply students with a highlighter pen and a wipe on/wipe off board. Any ideas that the student has while listening to a lesson can be written down, and the highlighter pen can be used to highlight key words in their own notebooks.

- Consider allocating a locker or drawer to each student as this will provide a place for them to put their larger possessions such as sports clothes and bags. This helps the student considerably; to have a base he or she can return to. It also helps to minimise the amount of equipment and books the student can potentially lose in different places around the school at one time. This can also reduce the level of anxiety and stress worrying about lost possessions.

Weekly Class Clean Up

A weekly class clean up can develop skills that can be transferred to home. It allows for time to check that equipment and books are put back in the correct place. The teacher can make sure that letters to home are not still sitting at the bottom of a student's bag! It teaches filing and sorting skills.

Ideas to help:

- With the students, identify a list of tasks for the whole class as well as personal tasks that the student needs to complete.
- Discuss how to prioritise tasks - what needs to be done now and what can wait till a later time.
- Have a rubbish bin available!

Staying on Task

Having a regular movement break can be useful for increasing attention and concentration. Stretching muscles when the student has been sitting for some time reduces muscle aches and tension, especially if the student has been working at a computer or writing for more than 30 minutes.

Ideas to help:

- Every 15-30 minutes of seated activities should incorporate a short movement break of 2-3 minutes.
- This can be done with the whole class and/or specific tasks can be given to students who need it more.
- If the student has been targeted specifically to need movement breaks, as they have difficulty attending and concentrating for a long period of time, try to make the movement break purposeful so they are not seen as different from their peers.

Movement Breaks

- Standing up to stretch 5 times and touch toes.

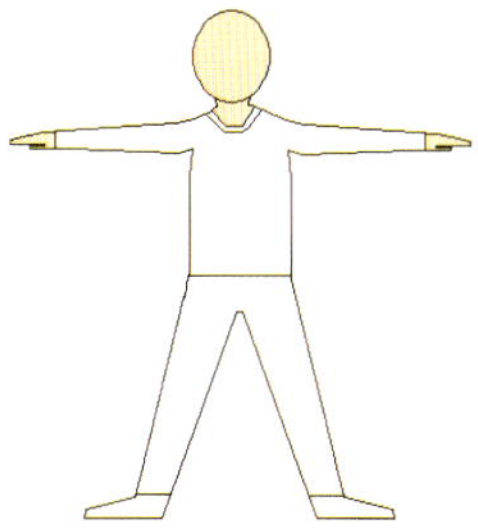

- Collecting a book from the shelf.

- Getting up from the chair and showing the teacher some work that has been completed.
- Pushing palms of hands together and pushing hard, (like in a 'praying' position) and linking fingers (monkey grip) and pulling (trying to pull them apart).

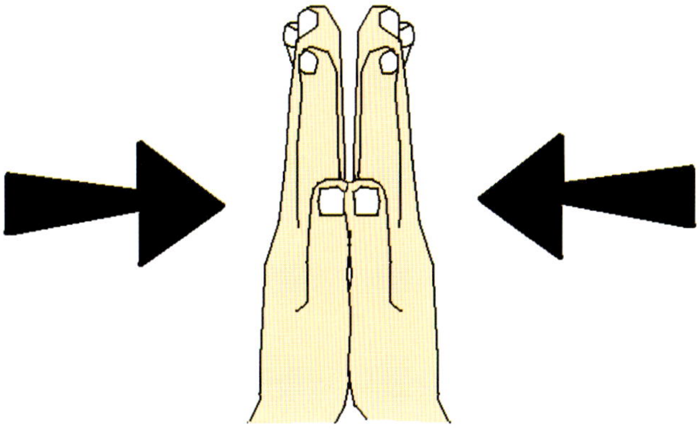

- If there is room in the classroom then the students can do floor push-ups. Sit cross-legged, place arms at sides. With palms resting on the floor, straighten arms to slowly lift body weight off the floor. Relax arms and return slowly to normal sitting.

- If there is less room in the classroom then chair push-ups may be a good idea. Sit on a chair, feet resting on the floor, grasp the sides of the chair near the front, shift the weight forward so that straight arms are supporting some body weight, and slowly bend elbows so that body weight is lowered. Discourage the student from bringing his or her weight too far forward so balance is lost.

- Shrugging shoulders - get the class to roll their shoulders forward and backwards. They can also look to the right and to the left, turning their head slowly.

- Playing the piano - get the class to play an imaginary piano on their desks with their fingers. Move from the thumbs and work both hands in unison. This can be done first quietly and slowly and then gradually speeding up and then slowing down again.

Breaking Tasks Down

It is useful to be able to analyse a task and know how to break it into parts in order to complete it step by step. This encourages the student to set goals and to see what he or she is aiming for and prioritise his or her actions.

Ideas to help:

- Show the student how you plan a task by talking it through with him or her. You could use an example such as making a cake or jam tarts, learning to ride a bike, writing an essay or learning to play a new or current sport such as football or netball.
- Use language such as:

  - what is required to start?

  - what is being aimed for in the end?

  - what equipment/tools are needed to do the task?

  - what is the next step?

  - how will you know when the task is completed?

One example of task analysis is playing football.

By getting the student to talk through all the aspects of the game, this allows a check as to whether he/she understands what he/she has to do.

1. What are the rules of the game?
2. What equipment is required e.g. balls?
3. What is the appropriate footwear?
4. How are the teams selected?
5. Where will the game be played?
6. What position will each student play?
7. Do you know what part you have to play in the game?
8. How will you know if you are winning or losing?
9. How long does the game last?
10. What are the correct "moves"?
11. How will you know when you have made a mistake? Role of the referee.
12. How will you know when the game is at an end? Whistle blows.
13. What happens after the game is finished? For example, collecting the ball, shaking hands with the other team, showering and changing.

General Tips:

- Your general approach to teaching organisational skills should be with **praise** and **encouragement**. New skills may need to be repeated often to be reinforced, and to alter old behaviours.
- Help the students to realise when they make good decisions by giving **focussed** feedback explaining what they have done well. For example:

"Well done.....by putting your homework straight into your bag you will remember it tonight."

- **Show students that talking strategies out loud** (but quietly) can help to reinforce actions.
- If the student has difficulties making decisions, help the student to **make a list of** 'pros' **and** 'cons'.

Photocopiable Resource

Things to do	Done

Timetable for

Stick Velcro here (day)

Subject	Time
Place Velcro strip here	
Morning break	
Place Velcro strip here	

Lunch	
Place Velcro strip here	
Afternoon break	
Place Velcro strip here	
Home time	

Monday	Tuesday
Wednesday	Thursday
Friday	Saturday
Sunday	

Monday	Tuesday
Wednesday	Thursday
Friday	Saturday
Sunday	

Sample pictures for class timetable

English

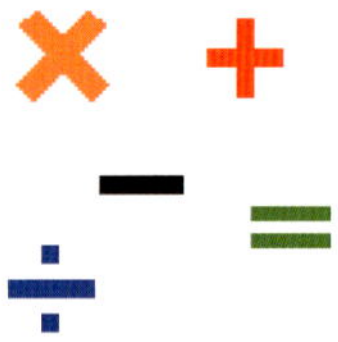

Maths

History

Registration

Art and craft

Reading

Geography

Assembly

Welsh

Reading

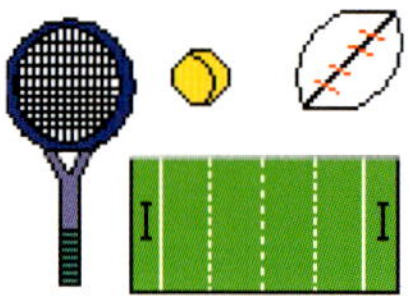

P.E.

Spelling

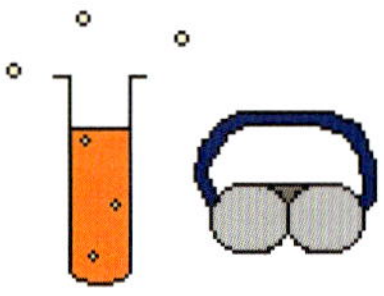

Science

Religious Studies

Useful Resources

Computer software

www.dyslexic.com

This company provides a range of software including concept mapping software such as Inspiration®, Kidspiration®, Mind Genius® and Mindfull®. In addition, study skills packages such as Timely Reminders®, and Wordswork® are also potentially helpful to the student. This site also contains games to help develop analytical skills and logical thinking such as 'Scally's World of Problems' and 'Thinkin' Things'.

www.clarosoftware.co.uk

This company has a range of free trial downloads of concept mapping software to try out. In addition text-to-speech software programmes that students can try to see if hearing what they have written helps.

http://www.mycorkboard.com

This is a freely downloadable personal organisation screen saver, which has Post-It® notes, a desktop calendar and clock (either in digital or analogue format).

Visual cookery websites

http://www.visualrecipes.com

http://homecooking.about.com

Many skills can be practised through cooking. For example, first thinking through and planning the task to be completed such as preparing the ingredients, then following the instructions in a logical sequence and seeing the outcome.

These websites help break down the activity into small steps and assist understanding through using pictures.

Games

http://www.happypuzzle.co.uk/

This company has a large selection of puzzles, games and toys which help with logical thinking, sequencing and planning. It also offers games to help with maths.

www.amazon.co.uk

Many games are available which help with step-by-step thinking (such as 'Cluedo®'), planning (such as 'Jenga®'), following instructions (such as building with 'Lego®'), turn-taking (such as 'Snakes and Ladders'), and sequencing and matching (such as 'Bingo').

Additional Organisational tips

http://www.wm.edu/ttac/articles/learning/orgskills.html

This site has additional organisational tips for assisting students.

http://stress.about.com/od/studentstress/Students_and_Stress_StudyHabits_Organization_Skills_Stress_Help.htm

This site contains articles relating to stress management and study skills for students.

http://www.3m.com/us/office/postit/digital/digital_notes.html

The Post-It® note site has free downloads for trial of Post- It® notes that can be placed on the desk top of the computer to help make to-do lists.